THE McGRAW-HILL AUTHOR'S BOOK

THE McGRAW-HILL AUTHOR'S BOOK

McGraw-Hill Book Company

New York
St. Louis
San Francisco
Toronto
London
Sydney

THE McGRAW-HILL AUTHOR'S BOOK

ISBN 07-045051-X

910111213 HDHD 898765432

TO OUR AUTHORS

Essentially, a publisher is the agent for its authors; those who create the publisher's products—its authors—are its chief assets and principal capital. McGraw-Hill is proud that it has been selected as editorial and marketing agent by thousands of distinguished scholars and authors in virtually every field of human endeavor.

As a publisher, McGraw-Hill has three major objectives:

1. To create and produce *instructional materials* for all levels—preschool programs, elementary schools, high schools, technical schools, colleges, universities, and postgraduate institutions
2. To create and produce *reference materials* for all professions and virtually all vocations—medicine, engineering, law, religion, science, business, education, and practical arts
3. To create and produce *materials that entertain, inspire, and inform*—works of fiction, humor, biography, religion, fine arts, and so on

And I do not confine my definition of materials to books. The term "materials" also includes films, tests, audiotapes, phonograph records, kits, programmed materials, instructional systems, charts, planetarium materials and equipment, and a host of other nonbook materials. Nor is our distribution of these materials limited to domestic markets; McGraw-Hill books, both English- and foreign-language editions, are sold throughout the world.

Thus, McGraw-Hill Book Company is dedicated to useful communication through all media and to all markets. It seeks to educate, inform, and entertain with honesty, relevance, and taste. In pursuing its objectives, McGraw-Hill supports purposeful inquiry and innovation, always searching for the new, the relevant. A basic characteristic of free enterprise is the right to speak freely and boldly; this right is defended vigorously at all times by McGraw-Hill in its own behalf and in behalf of its authors.

If you are a new author who has not published with us before, I welcome you to McGraw-Hill. I hope that your "brainchild" will be exactly as you wish it to be—distinguished in content, attractive in appearance, and successful in the marketplace. If you are already a McGraw-Hill author, may I express our gratitude for the opportunity to continue our association.

President
McGraw-Hill Book Company

CONTENTS

Preparing a Revision   57

How We Market Your Book   65

This Is McGraw-Hill   69

THE
McGRAW-HILL
AUTHOR'S
BOOK

THE
PUBLISHING
PARTNERSHIP

THE PUBLISHING PARTNERSHIP

Once we have reached an agreement—you to write a book and we to publish it—we are partners in an important undertaking, and our objective is the same: to produce a book that will reach the widest possible market and gain for us the confidence and respect of its users. We live by our names, and our books make our names.

The purpose of this volume is to help you produce the best possible manuscript so that together we can produce the best possible book. The success of our venture depends on how well both of us—the author and the publisher—do our jobs.

The Role of the Editor

The publisher's representative in working with the author is the editor. The term editor is applied to a number of people whose responsibilities vary widely. Basically, there are two types of editors: those who manage a publishing program (referred to here as *sponsoring editors*) and those who check manuscripts for accuracy, "style" them, and help transform them into printed pages (referred to here as *editing supervisors*).

The Sponsoring Editor

The sponsoring editor is responsible for managing a publishing program. (Sometimes he is called an executive editor, a senior editor, or a project director.) In the typical large publishing house, there are often one or more sponsoring editors for each major discipline and for each level. For example, in McGraw-Hill there is at least one sponsoring editor for elementary school English, another for high school English, and still another for college English. The same is true for mathematics, science, foreign languages, music, and so on. It is the sponsoring editor's responsibility to plan and publish as many books as are needed to serve his particular market. To do this, he must keep constantly in touch with current subject-matter developments and market trends. He talks to professors, curriculum groups, educators, and other leading people in the field; attends major conventions; reads widely; and carries on continuous editorial and marketing research.

Some sponsoring editors are subject-matter specialists themselves, particularly in elementary and high school book departments. More often than not, these editors are experienced teachers and writers, and they are capable of helping authors plan books—and even of helping to write them when the situation demands it. For example, the sponsoring editor for high school mathematics is likely to have taught mathematics for several years, to have contributed to professional journals, and perhaps to have written one or more successful mathematics books. Such an editor reads all manuscripts submitted in his subject area.

The Editing Supervisor

The editor who actually shepherds a manuscript from typescript to finished book is called an editing supervisor. (Other publishing houses may call him a production editor.) The typical editing supervisor is an English major (many have advanced degrees in English and have taught the subject) and has had several years of experience in producing books.

McGraw-Hill supervisors have almost unlimited resources to aid them in their work—excellent libraries (including a first-rate company library), over fifty professional and technical periodicals published by McGraw-Hill, and more than ten in-house publishing departments with specialties ranging from motion-picture films to medical textbooks. The company runs one of the industry's most effective training programs for editing personnel.

The editing supervisor, or a copy editor working under his supervision, goes over the manuscript very carefully, often several times. He tightens up loose sentences to make them clear and direct; guards against redundancies, contradictions, and inconsistencies; corrects grammar and usage; and establishes uniformity in capitalization, spelling, abbreviation, and other points of style. Some supervisors plan and gather illustrations, reorganize and rewrite copy (with the approval of the sponsoring editor and the author), figure out ways to display tables and charts, and supervise art and design.

The Role of the Designer

Every book has a character of its own, and it is up to the book designer—with his knowledge of art, typography, and printing processes—to capture that character. The designer selects the typefaces, chooses colors, determines layout, and supervises the preparation of the illustrations and the cover. He works toward two primary objectives: to make the book appealing to the potential customer and to make it easy to use. Ease of use is especially important in the design of textbooks, handbooks, and reference books.

The Role of the Production Specialist

Of equal importance to editors and designers are the production specialists—men who know printing processes and equipment, paper, binding methods, cost control, and scheduling. They constantly advise the editor on the best way to produce books of the highest quality at the lowest cost and with the greatest speed.

The Help You Will Receive

Before starting your book, you should discuss the following points with your editor. He will consult production specialists, designers, and others and provide you with the appropriate information.

1. Approximate size of your book and how to estimate the number of manuscript pages that will enable you to stay within the boundaries agreed upon
2. Physical preparation of your manuscript—how it should be typed, what rules of style and usage to follow, etc.
3. Schedule for completion of the manuscript
4. Methods of gathering and preparing illustrations
5. Organization of the manuscript for maximum usefulness to users
6. Contractual matters—royalties; allowable corrections in proof; obligation, if any, to prepare manuals and revisions; permissions and copyrights; assignment of the contract; and so on
7. Preparation of correlated and supplemental materials such as teachers' editions, films, filmstrips, transparencies, classroom equipment, and tests

GATHERING
MATERIALS
AND
WRITING
THE
MANUSCRIPT

GATHERING MATERIALS AND
WRITING THE MANUSCRIPT

Writing a book is an ambitious task. Although you may need no instructions on how to go about organizing yourself for completing the job, most new authors welcome some suggestions. The following hints are based on the methods used by many experienced McGraw-Hill authors.

Organization of Source Material

Most people who write books are "collectors" at heart. Over the years you may have collected lecture notes, newspaper and magazine articles, graphs, cartoons, tables, reports, bulletins, convention proceedings, and other types of printed materials. After you have made a rough outline of your book, set up a folder for each chapter or unit and sort your resource materials by topic. You will want to provide cross references when the material applies to more than one chapter.

As you keep up with your professional reading, have an 8½ by 11 pad handy for notes, and drop your notes in the appropriate chapter folder. Make sure you show the source of your notes, including author, name of book or periodical, volume number, date, and page number. Then you will not have to go back later for this information in case you have quoted from the material.

If you are writing a book in which fictitious names of people are used (as in law cases, problems, vignettes, and examples), keep a record for yourself of all the names you have used. One successful McGraw-Hill author puts each name on a 3 by 5 card; as he prepares a new story or case, he refers to his cards to make sure that he doesn't repeat a name and that he has a good balance of names of various national origins.

Reference Books

Most authors find it necessary to refresh their memory from time to time on spelling, grammar, and the correct use of words. The following works are recommended for your personal reference library.

Spelling

The current edition of Merriam-Webster's *New International Dictionary* (unabridged) is McGraw-Hill's general guide for spelling. We suggest that you refer to this (or the latest Merriam-Webster *Collegiate*) as you prepare your manuscript.

6

Grammar and Usage

A good grammar book is indispensable; there are many from which to choose. Among the most highly regarded works on usage are Fowler's *Modern English Usage* (edited by Sir Ernest Gowers, Oxford); Follett's *Modern American Usage* (Hill and Wang); Partridge's *Usage and Abusage* (Penguin); and Perrin's *Writer's Guide and Index to English* (Scott, Foresman). Many authors also find it helpful to refer to a book of synonyms, such as *Roget's Thesaurus* (Crowell).

Writing Refresher

If your writing is a little rusty, we suggest that you read the brief but highly regarded *Elements of Style* by Strunk and White (Macmillan).

Style

Style, in publishing, refers to the consistent use of an accepted standard for punctuation, capitalization, abbreviation, footnote and bibliographic form, the writing of numbers, and so on. We urge you to adopt uniform and well-established forms in preparing your manuscript; we shall be happy to advise you on matters of style at any stage of preparation.

Rules of style acceptable in one discipline may not apply in another. Most publishers combine the best-established usages to form their own "house style." McGraw-Hill style standards are respected throughout the publishing world. They are high standards that have evolved over the years through constant contact with authors, style authorities, scientific and technical organizations, professional associations, and so on. Our editors keep up to date with changes in style and adjust McGraw-Hill's standards whenever the changes appear to be well founded and likely to endure.

Writing Procedures

Before starting to write, some authors outline the chapter in minute detail and then revise the outline over and over. This is no doubt the best method for achieving good organization, proper coverage, and continuity. Some writers prepare only a broad list of topics they plan to cover and start immediately to write. In other words, they don't know what they want to say until they have tried to say it! Although this may not seem efficient, it works quite well for some people. Of course, these authors will rewrite their chapters more often than the careful organizer.

Rewrite!

Regardless of the way in which you approach your writing task, be prepared to rewrite and polish several times. Even the experienced author may rewrite his first draft of a chapter a half dozen times before it satisfies him. If you find that you have difficulty putting your ideas down smoothly on the first, second, or even third try, don't despair—most successful authors go over their drafts many, many times.

The Publisher Can Help

When you have written two or three chapters of your manuscript, send them to your editor. Our specialists will examine the material carefully and, where appropriate, make suggestions that will save you time and result in faster production of your book.

Reading Level

In many books—elementary school, high school, and introductory college textbooks, for example—reading level is extremely important and is carefully controlled. Make sure you are not writing above the heads of your readers. There are several "readability formulas" you can use. One of the easiest to use is the *Dale-Chall Formula for Predicting Readability,* which can be obtained from the Ohio State University Press for about 50 cents.

Selection of Illustrations

Most textbooks are fairly heavily illustrated—photographs, diagrams, maps, flow charts, drawings, cartoons, and so on—and you and your editor will decide early in the game the number and type of illustrations to be included in your book and the extent of your responsibility for them.

Any illustrations you supply should, of course, be clear and sharp. Photographs should be high-contrast glossy prints or original film—not cutouts from newspapers and magazines. Drawings should be in black ink and cleanly executed.

If you are to supply the illustrations, you can obtain free ones from a number of sources—business firms like Du Pont, United States Steel, and International Business Machines; city, state, and federal government agencies; schools and universities; community organizations; libraries; and philanthropic groups.

Some sources charge a fee for their illustrations. These include commercial agencies such as Monkmeyer, Black Star, A. Devaney, and Pictograph; publishers of newspapers, magazines, and books; art agencies; and professional artists and photographers. When you purchase an illustration, you must remember that its use is limited to one book; if you expect to use it in another book or in a new edition, you must pay an additional fee.

Identify Your Sources

Most suppliers of illustrations—both free and commercial—require a credit line in the book in which their pictures are used, and you must identify your sources when you submit illustrations. If your pictures have legends (captions), credit may be given in parentheses at the end of each legend, as necessary.

Keep Illustrations Separate

Keep your illustrations separate from the manuscript. Set up an illustration folder for each chapter so that as you come across ideas in magazines, newspapers, and other sources, you can file them easily.

The Size of Your Book

In the early planning stages of your book, you will have an understanding with your editor about the number of pages the finished book will contain. Until the dimensions and design of the book have been determined, however, it is very difficult to estimate whether you are writing more material for each chapter than you need. The formulas for converting manuscript pages to printed book pages are complicated and difficult to apply, but your editor will be glad to give you a rough guide for estimating length if you send him a few chapters as soon as they are finished. Cutting a manuscript after it has been completed is a painful task for both editor and author and costly in time for everyone.

Student Activity Material

If you are writing a textbook, you will probably wish to include student activity material at the end of each learning segment. These activities consist of vocabulary reviews, questions on the chapter, problems and projects, cases, and the like. Write this material as soon as you have written the chapter itself. If you wait until the manuscript is finished, you are likely to gloss over or skip some major points. Remember, many teachers consider the student activity material just as important as the text matter (especially in el-hi books), and so the exercises should be thoughtfully and carefully prepared.

Preparing Answers to Student Activity Material

At the time you write the student activity material, make a key (answers) to it. There are two important reasons for preparing answers at this time:

1. The job will be easier because the material is fresh in your mind.
2. You will know at once whether the material is appropriate. (Authors who wait until the book is set in type before preparing the key sometimes find that they have to go back and change questions and problems in proof—they discover too late that some of the questions can't be answered!)

Workbooks and Other Supplements

You will have an understanding with your editor early in your project about whether you are expected to prepare a workbook, study guide, test booklet, or other items to support your textbook.

The Workbook or Study Guide

If a workbook or study guide is to accompany your text, prepare it at the same time that you are writing the text. We suggest this because as you do the workbook, you are likely to want to change your textbook content occasionally to fit some of your workbook ideas. If the workbook is to tie in with the text on a chapter-by-chapter basis, prepare it when you have finished your student activity materials in the text. Do the key to the workbook at the same time.

Other Instructional Aids

Today, authors are often encouraged to develop student and teacher aids to be sold in support of their books—aids such as transparencies, filmstrips, tapes, records, and flip charts. If you have ideas for such instructional aids, your editor will be glad to hear about them. Make your plans for these aids as early as possible so that as you write your textbook and other supplements, you can be thinking of content and illustrations that lend themselves to audio or visual treatment.

Teacher's Manuals

Many el-hi and introductory college textbooks owe much of their success to helpful manuals for the teacher. The typical teacher's manual contains answers to the student activities in the textbook and its supplements, as well as ideas for teaching the course, lists of audio-visual aids, bulletin-board suggestions, bonus problems and activities, sources of free and inexpensive pamphlet material, and so on. As you write each chapter, jot down the ideas that occur to you for the teacher's manual. Don't put off the job until the book is done; there is always a clamor for the manual immediately upon publication of the textbook.

Budgeting Your Time

The faster you produce a good manuscript, the more quickly it can be published. You and your editor will come to an agreement early about the date the complete manuscript is to be submitted. Although the editor will want your manuscript as quickly as you can produce it, he will not expect you to sacrifice quality for the sake of speed.

Make a Schedule

It's a good idea to set up your schedule in terms of chapters. A year and a half may seem a long time for writing a thirty-six-chapter book, but when you break the job down by chapters, you realize that the schedule calls for two chapters a month. And if you also have a workbook, a teacher's manual, and other supplements to prepare, your schedule must allow for these, too.

Budget Daily Writing Time

Some authors are like some students—they put off the job until the last minute, telling themselves that they have a semester break or a summer vacation coming up. A last-minute manuscript is nearly always written in a frenzy, resulting in a hastily constructed, poorly organized piece of work that doesn't please the author and puts an extra burden on the publisher—usually delaying the publication of the book.

When you are ready to start writing, begin immediately to budget your time, setting aside specific hours during *each day* when you can hang the "Do Not Disturb" sign outside your door. Until the job is finished, you have to expect to work at it not only during the day but evenings, weekends, and vacations as well.

Delays Are Costly

Delay in submitting your manuscript usually means a later publication date for the book. The ideal time to bring out a book is around the first of January: the book has a current copyright date, and the publisher has several months before school closes to promote it and present it to textbook committees and instructors for fall use. The delay of even a few weeks can make the book come out too late for effective promotion and selling.

One of the reasons why a delayed manuscript often means a later publication date is that most printers must schedule the manufacturing of a book months in advance. When one manuscript is not ready to go into its scheduled "time slot," another is dropped into its place.

Files and Correspondence

A four-drawer filing cabinet is a good investment. (We know some authors who have three or four.) If you are writing an elementary or high school textbook, you may find when it's all over that the correspondence with your editor weighs about as much as the manuscript!

Set up an efficient procedure for filing manuscript copy, illustrations, and correspondence. When you write your editor or coauthor, make sure you keep a copy of your letter. You'll have frequent occasion to refer to previous correspondence.

Keep in Touch with Your Editor

Your editor likes to have frequent progress reports from you, even when you have no "progress" to report. Make it a point to keep him posted on how you are getting on with your writing and whether you are staying on schedule. He can plan the production of your book better when he knows the exact date the manuscript will be in, and he can feed advance information to the sales and promotion people so that they can get a head start on advertising and other preselling activities.

Minority Groups

Like most other educational publishers, McGraw-Hill has a policy of publishing textbooks and other instructional materials that truly reflect the society in which we live. This includes accurate and fair representation of minority groups and their role in America today. Specifically, this policy is:

1. American Negroes and other minorities should be represented in instructional materials, in both content and illustration, on the same basis as other groups. We are committed to fully integrated learning materials for the pluralistic society in which we live.
2. In subjects such as history and social studies, we encourage forthright discussions of the economic, political, social, and moral questions relating to intergroup relations.
3. We will not publish an alternative version of any book, film, or other educational medium in order to sell it to institutions that do not wish to use integrated materials.

This policy can be stated here only in broad terms, of course, and the author will want to discuss it fully with his editor—if possible while the book is in the early planning stages.

PERMISSIONS
AND
COPYRIGHTS

PERMISSIONS AND COPYRIGHTS

You must give credit to the copyright holder for any material you quote or adapt from copyrighted sources, and you are responsible for obtaining permission for its use in your book. Write to the holder of the original copyright, not to a secondary source. A recommended form for requesting permission for use of ordinary quotations is shown in Figure 1. If you wish to reproduce complete articles or works of literature, however, you will have to give the copyright holder more specific information about how you intend to use the material. You can save a good deal of time if you will ask for permission to use the material in future revisions as well as in the current edition.

The penalties for infringement of copyright are severe and are not to be risked lightly, but the boundaries beyond which you may not trespass are indistinct. Our own rule of thumb is to get permission in writing for quotations or slightly paraphrased adaptations of more than four printed lines (about forty or fifty words).

It is just as important to get permission from publishers of newspapers, magazines, pamphlets, and bulletins as it is from publishers of books. Permission must also be obtained for the use of tables, music, illustrations, and advertisements. Dictionary publishers are particularly strict on the use of their copyrighted definitions, and you must get permission for even the briefest excerpt.

Send two copies of your permission request letter to the copyright owner, asking him to return one signed copy for your files.

United States Government Publications

Although many United States government publications are not copyrighted, you should obtain permission to take material from them. These publications often contain previously copyrighted material, and inclusion in government publications does not nullify subsisting copyrights.

Lecture Notes

You may unwittingly lay yourself open to a charge of copyright infringement when preparing a book based on a series of lectures you have given or on a symposium in which you have participated. Your notes, compiled from various sources at a time when you had no thought of publication, may not contain data about the sources you drew upon; and when you start writing your book, you may forget that some of the material is borrowed from others. It is important to retrace the path of your original research in order to obtain the necessary permissions and give the proper credit.

Gentlemen:

I am preparing a textbook tentatively entitled [Title]
to be published by McGraw-Hill Book Company in [probable date]
and intended for use by [freshmen, graduate students,
physicians, etc.].

I should like your permission to reproduce in my book,
and in its future editions, the material indicated below.

Author(s):

Title and date of publication:

Selection: [first and last words if a quotation]

From page_____to page_____

Approximate number of words_____or pages_____

It is understood, of course, that full credit will
be given to the author and publisher, either as a footnote
or as a reference within the text, or both.

A release form is given below for your convenience.
The duplicate copy of this request is for your files.

Very truly yours,

[Name, title, etc.]

. . . .

Permission is granted for use of the material as
stipulated.

Date _____   _____
                                        Signature

                                        _____
                                        Title

Figure 1. Letter requesting permission.

Illustrations

If you plan to include illustrations borrowed from other sources (tables, charts, cartoons, advertisements, photographs—just about everything you pick up for use), make sure you obtain written permission for them. You must assume that permission is required even though the material doesn't appear to be copyrighted. When you plan to revise or adapt an illustration for your own use, it is also wise to obtain permission to do so.

When you use a photograph of a living person, obtain his permission in writing first. Failure to do so may be very costly indeed. If you are the photographer, you must be especially careful to get a written release from the subject even if he is a personal friend. To make the release binding, pay the subject a consideration, even if only a dollar, for rights to use the picture in the text and for advertising and trade purposes relating to it.

Photographs that you obtain from commercial sources may not be used until they are paid for. The release for these photographs and those you obtain from business firms is usually stamped on the back. Incidentally, permission to use a photograph in a textbook does not extend to its use in advertising; another release must be obtained for this purpose.

Beware of Libel

Don't use the names of friends and relatives in your book, even though your reference to them may appear harmless. One author, in citing a case of fraud, used the name of a friend as the guilty party. Later when the author and his friend had a falling out, suit for libel was threatened.

Care should always be taken to avoid defamatory statements about a person—accusing him of a crime, holding him up to ridicule, or attempting to injure him in his trade, business, or profession.

Also, be careful not to slur racial, religious, or professional groups in your text or in the illustrations. On one occasion suit was threatened when the author of a consumer book called a certain group of non-M.D.'s a "cult."

Duration of Copyright

You can assume that a work is protected by copyright for fifty-six years if renewal has been obtained. A revision of the present domestic copyright law is under consideration by Congress; if the bill is passed, many of the existing concepts of the law, including the period of protection, will change.

Most textbooks, handbooks, and reference books are copyrighted in the name of the publisher, and it is his responsibility to keep the copyright up to date. If after a certain period of time the decision is made to declare the book out of print, the publisher notifies the author and may offer to reassign the copyright to him. If such assignment is made to the author, he then assumes the responsibility for renewing the copyright.

Start Early

If you start writing for permissions in the early stages of preparing your manuscript, you will have them all cleared by the time you send the manuscript to us. We can't start setting your manuscript in type until we have assurance that your permissions have been obtained.

   If you have questions on copyrights and permissions, write to your editor. McGraw-Hill has a Permissions and Copyrights Department, as well as a staff of legal specialists, and the counsel of these people is available to our authors.

PREPARING
THE
MANUSCRIPT
FOR
THE
PUBLISHER

PREPARING THE MANUSCRIPT FOR THE PUBLISHER

As you are drafting and revising your manuscript, questions on the practical aspects of manuscript preparation will frequently come up. Here are answers to some of the questions most often raised.

Paper

Use a good quality of white bond paper, $8\frac{1}{2}$ by 11 inches. Test it to be sure it will take corrections in fountain-pen ink without "feathering." The publisher prefers a bond stock with some rag content, 16- to 20-pound weight.

Please don't use flimsy paper like onionskin or tissue. Manuscripts are handled many times by editors, compositors, and proofreaders; a soft or flimsy paper is soon reduced to tatters.

And please, *please* avoid the erasable bond papers, which are sold under various trade names. They are not suitable for manuscripts because:

1. They have a coating to which ink does not adhere.
2. Some of them are brittle, like parchment, and will disintegrate before the production process is finished.
3. The type is too easily eradicated—by ink eradicator, printer's chemicals, an ordinary eraser, or just plain handling.

Mechanics of Typing

1. Double-space all copy, including footnotes, excerpts from other authors, and tables. Use only one side of the sheet.
2. Leave at least a $1\frac{1}{2}$-inch margin on all sides, to allow space for the editor's and printer's markings.
3. Use the same size of typewriter type throughout.
4. Try to keep the width of your typed lines and the number of lines to a page fairly uniform throughout the manuscript. This helps us to estimate more quickly the number of pages in the finished book.
5. Use a black noneradicable ribbon. Change the ribbon often so that you always get a good black impression. With all the handling your manuscript will get, a faint typing impression soon becomes illegible.
6. Clean the typewriter keys (type bars) frequently. Clogged keys make it hard to distinguish o's from e's.

20

Duplicated Copy

We would rather you didn't submit mimeographed, Ditto, or photostatic copy. Too often the copy is faint, the paper doesn't take corrections well, and the material is single-spaced.

Numbering the Pages

Number the pages of your manuscript in the upper right corner. You may number them by chapter (*5–1, 5–2,* etc.) while the manuscript is in preparation; when it is finished, however, the pages should be numbered consecutively throughout.

If you want to insert one or more sheets after your manuscript has been paged, give the insertions the number of the preceding page, with *a, b, c,* etc., added; for example, *121a, 121b, 121c.* To avoid loss of *a* pages, write on page 121: *121a, 121b, and 121c follow.*

If you remove a page, you can double-number the preceding page; for example, *83 and 84.* If you take out several pages, you can show the omission as follows: *83–87.* This goes on the page that precedes the removed pages.

Inserts and Corrections

Occasionally you will want to make insertions in your manuscript after it has been typed. Minor corrections and addition of a few words may be made in the space above the line where the material applies. Type the insertions or use ink. Don't make your insertions in the margin; the editor needs this space for notes and marks for the compositor.

Minor Corrections

Figure 2 illustrates minor corrections made by the author after the manuscript has been typed. Of course, if a great many minor corrections are inserted on a

Figure 2. *Minor corrections in manuscript.*

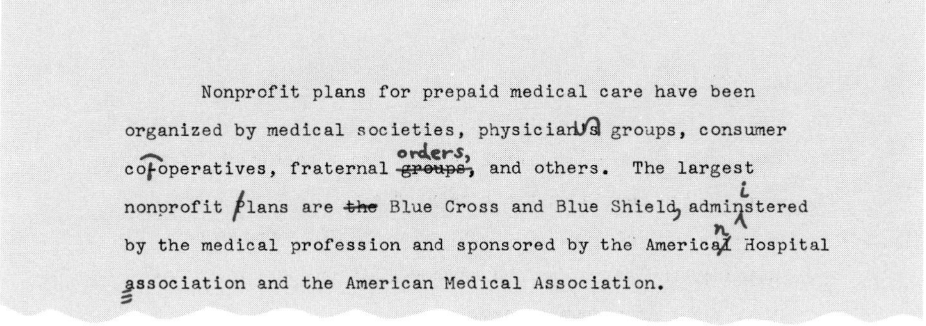
Nonprofit plans for prepaid medical care have been organized by medical societies, physicians' groups, consumer coöperatives, fraternal ~~groups,~~ orders, and others. The largest nonprofit plans are ~~the~~ Blue Cross and Blue Shield, administered by the medical profession and sponsored by the American Hospital Association and the American Medical Association.

page, the printer may have a major problem (for which he often penalizes the publisher); it is best to retype heavily corrected pages.

Longer Insertions

Longer insertions should be typed on a full-sized sheet of paper and added as an *a* page to the manuscript (see Figure 3). Indicate where the insertion is to be placed by noting "Insert A [page number]." On the insert itself, write in bold print "This is Insert A."

Don'ts for Insertions and Corrections

Here are three important don'ts for handling insertions and corrections:

1. Don't make insertions on fliers that increase the length or width of the

Figure 3.   Making an insert.

190

> Many people use the same basic reason to rationalize bad listening. When someone talks to them, they mentally criticize either physical appearance or speech delivery, or both. Perhaps the speaker has a speech defect, such as a bad lisp, or has a foreign accent. The defects become excuses for not listening.

Insert Ⓐ from p. 190a >   This is not to intimate that physical appearances and manners of speech have nothing to do with what you hear. They do. They may tell you a great deal about the speaker, but

190a

This is insert Ⓐ

"A person who talks like that can't have much to say," assumes the person on the receiving end. Or the listener becomes too critical of clothing, cosmetics, shoeshines, hairdos, and so on, and he assumes, "Anyone who looks like that can't have much to say."

typewritten sheet (8½ by 11). Dangling edges have a way of getting mutilated and sometimes torn off.

2. Don't write an insert in a streamer up the margin, forcing the printer to remove the page from his holding device, turn it sideways, and puzzle over it as he sets the material.

3. Don't write an insert on the back of the page, where it will probably be overlooked.

Mounted Copy

If you are submitting tear sheets from other printed materials, trim and mount them on 8½ by 11 sheets. If the material doesn't fit on a standard manuscript page, it is best to retype it.

In mounting any kind of copy—tear sheets, insertions, and the like—always use rubber cement. Never use cellophane tape, paper clips, or staples.

Chapter Title

A chapter or unit should always begin on a new page, and the title should be centered at least 1½ inches from the top of the page and typed in capital letters.

In the interest of attractive design, try to avoid a heading at the start of a chapter where it will follow directly below the chapter title. Your book will look better if you have at least one paragraph of copy before your first head (see Figure 4).

Figure 4.   Typing the chapter opening.

```
              CHAPTER 17.   INTERNATIONAL TRADE


        Trade among countries is called international trade.
   From the point of view of any one country, the trade its people
   carry on with people of other countries is its foreign trade.
   IMPORTANCE OF FOREIGN TRADE
        The people of the United States would find it extremely
   difficult, if not impossible, to get along without foreign
```

Style of Headings

Textbooks and reference books usually have a generous number of headings. Headings break up copy and guide the reader. But don't overdo it in terms of *variety* of headings; most well-organized textbooks need no more than three or four ranks (levels) of headings. Too many ranks of headings clutter a book's appearance and confuse the reader.

In typing your manuscript, follow a consistent style of positioning the headings to indicate their levels. An acceptable pattern is shown in Figure 5.

If you discover that your typist has not typed your headings according to the proper degree, go back over the entire manuscript and indicate which value you intend each heading to have. Write No. 1, No. 2, etc., in the left margin beside the heading, and circle the number.

The use of a consistent pattern of headings in the manuscript reduces the chances of error in transforming them into print. The designer will display the headings typographically according to the values you have indicated. He has the

Figure 5.   Typing the headings.

```
                    CHAPTER 1.  THIS IS THE CHAPTER TITLE


          The chapter title is centered and capitalized.

     THIS IS THE NUMBER 1 HEAD
          The number 1 head is flush left on a separate line.
     All the letters are capitalized.


     This Is the Number 2 Head
          The number 2 head is flush left on a separate line
     and underlined.  The main words begin with capital letters.


          This Is the Number 3 Head.  The number 3 head is
     paragraph-indented, and the copy "runs in" (follows on the
     same line).  Like the number 2 head, it is underlined,
     and the main words begin with capital letters.


          This is the number 4 head.  The number 4 head is
     like the number 3 head except that only the first letter
     is capitalized.
```

advantage of a great many display typefaces and sizes from which to choose, and he may elect to space or indent the heads in a variety of ways. In some books, color may be used to add emphasis to certain levels of headings.

Tables

Often a table (see Figure 6) is the best way to illustrate a point or present certain essential information. A good table enables the reader to grasp a concept very quickly. Make sure your tables meet this criterion; some tables confuse rather than help the reader.

Figure 6.   *A well-typed table.*

Table 1.2. Productivity of Recently Cut Commercial

Forest Land in the United States, Including

Coastal Alaska

Type of ownership	Total commercial forest land, million acres	Operating area,* million acres	Operating area by productivity classes, percent		
			Upper level	Middle level	Lower level
Private:					
Forest industries[†]....	62	44	77	19	4
Farm.................	165	53	41	37	22
Other private.........	131	42	52	28	20
Public.................	131	96	80	17	3
Total.................	489	235			

*Field examinations limited to operating units in which cutting had taken place from Jan. 1, 1947, through 1953.

[†]The pulp and paper group leads with an average of 84 percent in the upper level.

Source: Kenneth P. Davis, *Forest Management*, 2d ed., McGraw-Hill Book Company, New York, 1966.

Double-number your tables by chapter and number within that chapter. Refer to the table by number; for example: "As shown in Table 6–3, the difference between. . . ."

Footnotes

In many college and professional books, footnotes are a "must." (They are not used very often in typical el-hi textbooks.)

The style of footnotes varies a good deal depending on the type of book you are writing, and complete instructions on footnotes for various types of books are furnished McGraw-Hill authors. Here are examples of footnote styles for typical nontechnical books.

Reference to a Book

[1] Francis J. Reithel, *Concepts in Biochemistry,* McGraw-Hill Book Company, New York, 1967, p. 69.

Reference to a Periodical

[2] Irving Kolodin, "The Genesis of the Inexplicable," *Saturday Review,* Mar. 26, 1967, p. 62.

Reference to a Serial Publication

[3] "Forestry as a Vocation," *Occupational Outlook Handbook,* U.S. Bureau of Labor Statistics Bulletin 998, 1951, p. 43.

Typing Footnotes

Type footnotes double-spaced, with ordinary paragraph indention, and place them either (1) at the foot of the page without rules or (2) in the body of the manuscript on the line below the text reference and separated from the text by rules above and below. The number referring to a footnote should appear both in the text at the point of reference and before the footnote. Footnotes may be numbered either by page or by chapter.

Table Footnotes

Table footnotes should be typed at the foot of the table and not at the foot of the page, where they might be confused with text footnotes (Figure 6). They should be keyed with the standard symbols, *, †, ‡, §, ¶, unless there are more than five. In that case, use superscript italic letters, *a, b, c, d, e, f,* etc., instead of superscript symbols. The source footnote comes last. *Never* number table footnotes in sequence with text footnotes, and do not use *ibid.* or *op. cit.* in a table to refer to text footnotes or to previous tables—repeat the reference in full.

Bibliographies

Some textbooks contain extensive bibliographies. The style of the bibliography should match that of footnotes, with two exceptions:

1. Names of authors are inverted (for ease of alphabetizing); when there are coauthors, the name of only the senior author is inverted.
2. A colon rather than a comma separates the author's name from the title.

Here is an example of a bibliographic entry:

Adrian, Charles R., and Charles Press: *The American Political Process*, McGraw-Hill Book Company, New York, 1965, pp. 109–114.

Small-type Material

Excerpts from published works that are longer than four or five lines are usually set in type smaller than that used for the body of the text. The same is true of cases, illustrative problems, and examples in the text. *Such material should be double-spaced like all other copy.* The extent of the material can be shown in one of two ways in the manuscript.

1. Starting on a new line, type the material to the same width as the text matter. Place a vertical line in the left margin, to indicate beginning and end (see Figure 7).

Figure 7.   *How to indicate small-type material by a line.*

```
the playground site into, under, and on top of the build-

ing.  Harold Gores describes this effort to provide city

schoolchildren with more refreshing surroundings:

        It is quite possible that some day this building in

    its high-rise setting will be literally alive from top to

    bottom with shrubs and flowers the children planted.  A

    sunflower, though eighty feet in the air, is still a sun-

    flower, and the big city could use a few to diminish its

    brassy, glassy facelessness.

        The tremendous potential of new instructional materials

    and technology has been recognized in the Committee's recommenda-
```

2. Starting on a new line, indent the first paragraph of the small-type material ten spaces, the remaining lines five spaces (see Figure 8).

Notice that in Figure 8 a short excerpt ("goods must be both existing and identified . . .") is run into the text with quotation marks.

Mathematical Material

If you are writing a technical book, one of your main problems is to express mathematical symbols so clearly and so exactly that the compositor cannot fail to recognize your intention. A separate pamphlet on the preparation of technical manuscripts is available to McGraw-Hill authors, and it may be obtained from your editor.

Illustrations

Numbering Illustrations

If there are very few illustrations in your book, they may be single-numbered (1, 2, 3, etc.) throughout. Otherwise double-number them (1–1, 1–2, etc.) by chapter. The first number identifies the chapter or unit; the second number, the illustration within that chapter or unit.

Figure 8. *How to indicate small-type material by indention.*

The Uniform Commercial Code provides that "goods must be both existing and identified before any interest in them can pass. Goods which are not both existing and identified are 'future goods.'"

    Dickerson decided to have a set of seat covers put on his new car. The covers were to be cut out of a bolt of material and made to fit the upholstery. Title to the seat covers would not pass to Dickerson until they had been finished and installed. The agreement was a contract to sell.

Ownership rights to personal property may be passed to a buyer without a money payment. Numerous credit sales are made

```
        In no case is the insurance company liable for more

    than the actual loss, even though the face of the policy

    is more than the actual loss.
```

```
        The maximum amount that will be paid by the insurance

    company is the replacement value of the property that is des-
```

Figure 9. *How to indicate an illustration in manuscript.*

Identifying Illustrations

For each illustration, show the title and edition of the book in which it is to be used, the name of the author, and the figure number. Place this identifying information on a separate sheet attached to the illustration.

Indicating Illustrations in Your Manuscript

Keep all illustration copy separate from the manuscript, and indicate in your manuscript where you wish an illustration to be placed (see Figure 9).

Line Drawings

If an artist or draftsman is preparing original drawings or charts for you, ask him to make them at least twice the size they will appear in the book, in order to give a sharper reproduction when they are reduced. A drawing before and after reduction is shown in Figure 10.

In general, try to have all original drawings prepared for a uniform scale of reduction (for example, twice the final reduced size); this will save a great deal of time and cost in producing your book. Remember to make the labels on your illustrations large enough so that they will not be too small to read when the illustrations are reduced.

Photographs

Here are four important don'ts in handling photographs.

1. Don't use paper clips directly on photographs. Protect the glossy print with heavy paper or light cardboard.
2. Don't write on the face or back of a photograph. If arrows, numbers, and letters must be used to indicate details that will be identified in the

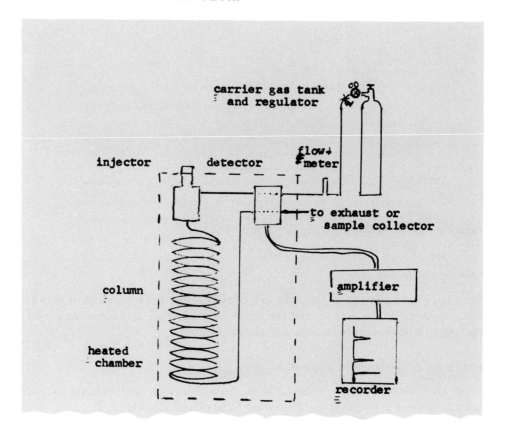

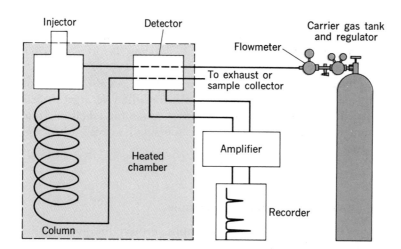

Figure 10. *Above, author's original sketch; below, draftsman's version, reduced to required size.*

legend, show them in the desired positions on an overlay (a tissue sheet attached to the back of the photograph with masking tape so that the tissue folds over to cover the face).

3. Even when writing on an overlay or a sheet attached to a photograph, don't use a lead pencil or a ball-point pen. The indentations will show up on the face of the photograph. It is best to write on a separate sheet of paper and *then* to attach it to the photograph.

4. Don't mount your photographs on heavy cardboard. Just cover them with a tissue overlay and leave them flat. If you obtain mounted photographs from outside sources, don't try to remove the photos from their backing; our experts will handle the job for you.

Care in Handling Illustrations

Handle all original illustration copy as though it were marked "Fragile." The slightest mark, crease, or indentation will show up in the reproduction. For shipping instructions, see page 33.

Legends

Legends (captions) for illustrations are set in type separately; therefore, if you are to supply legends, submit them in list form on $8\frac{1}{2}$ by 11 paper, double-spaced. Supply two copies. Number the legends to correspond to the numbered illustrations. Don't include the legend copy in the manuscript; use only the number or identifying caption as shown in Figure 9.

Front Matter

Besides the copyright notice (which we provide), the front matter of your book will include at least a title page, a preface, and a table of contents. Forewords are increasingly rare in textbooks, but may be included if desired.

The Title Page

The title page of your manuscript should show the name of your book, your name and degree (the degree may or may not be shown in the printed book), and your present affiliation. For example:

THE RETAIL MANAGER

Claude C. Calhoun, Ph.D.
Professor of Marketing
Michigan State University

A trend in el-hi textbooks is to include on the title page or elsewhere in the front matter a short biographical sketch of the author, and you may be asked to supply one. Here is a typical biographical sketch from a McGraw-Hill book:

> Seth A. Fessenden is Chairman of the Department of Speech at California State College at Fullerton. His teaching experience covers more than thirty years, starting in high school at Carbondale, Illinois. He has taught at Cornell College, The University of Denver, and Montana State University. Dr. Fessenden serves as Educational Research Consultant for Toastmasters International and is author and coauthor of many books and articles, among them *Speech and the Teacher, The Listener's Manual,* and *Understanding and Being Understood.* He is a member of principal speech and communications associations and frequently appears on convention programs.

The Preface

The aim of the preface is to establish the purpose and scope of your book. It should be given as careful thought as the content of the book itself.

Try to make your preface interesting, remembering that both the instructor and the student are likely to read it. Tell why your book was written, how it differs from others on the subject, what its main features are, for whom it is intended, how it is organized, and how it may be used most effectively. You can write a better preface if you will remember (1) that the prospective user of your book often looks there first to see whether your work and his need coincide and (2) that the representative trying to sell your book looks there for the points he can emphasize to prospective users. While you don't want the preface to sound like advertising copy, neither do you want it to be dull and lifeless or to sound like a dissertation.

Most authors receive special help in preparing their manuscripts—from people who provided illustrations, read and criticized the manuscript, supplied source data, and so on. The place to acknowledge this help is at the end of the preface. By all means, acknowledge everyone (making sure you have the correct full name, title, and affiliation), but don't overdo it. Although we greatly appreciate the thought, we ask you not to acknowledge help you receive from your McGraw-Hill editor or from our staff. Even though it may seem to you that they went beyond the call of duty, they don't look at it that way.

The Table of Contents

You and your editor will determine how detailed the table of contents should be. For some books, a list of chapter titles and page numbers is sufficient; for others, major topics, units, or sections of chapters are also listed.

While the table of contents is an important reference for the reader (especially the teacher), it is also often a selling feature of the book. Many teachers turn to the table of contents first when examining a new book because it gives them a quick view of the coverage. It should therefore be attractive and readable.

At the time you type your table of contents you won't know, of course, the book page on which each chapter begins. Leave the page references blank; the editing supervisor will insert them when the book is made up.

Other Elements of Front Matter

Most textbooks contain only a title page, a preface, a table of contents, and possibly a foreword in the front matter. However, your book may require other elements, as follows:

List of Illustrations.   In some types of books (a geography book, for example), it is helpful to the teacher and student to have a list of the maps, tables, and other important illustrations.

Dedication.   A dedication page is sometimes used in textbooks; and when space permits, we are always glad to include one. Most dedications are brief: "For Tommy and Meg," for example.

Shipping the Manuscript

In some cases you will be asked to submit your manuscript chapter by chapter as it is completed. In this way, the editor, designer, and illustrator can begin their work earlier. Small segments of manuscript copy are usually put in a kraft envelope and sent by first-class mail. Large, bulky manuscripts should be protected with cardboard and wrapped securely; they are usually sent by parcel post.

Please don't staple the pages of your manuscript. If you want to separate the units or chapters, put them in manila folders.

Shipping Illustrations

Photographs should be shipped flat, with cardboard stiffeners top and bottom, and clearly marked "Photos—Do Not Bend." All illustration copy should be protected by strong, oversized cardboard backing to prevent bending or crumpling in transit (corners are especially vulnerable).

Insurance

Don't forget to insure the manuscript for an amount that would enable you to have the copy retyped from your carbon; illustrations, for an amount that would enable you to replace them.

Keep Copies of Everything

Although we mentioned it earlier, we want to emphasize the importance of keeping a clear copy of your manuscript, including insertions and corrections you made on the original you are sending to us. Also, it's a good idea to have some kind of record of the illustrations you supply—copies, if possible.

THE
PRODUCTION
PROCESS

THE PRODUCTION PROCESS

The procedure for editing, designing, illustrating, and printing your book varies somewhat according to the kind of book you have written. For example, the steps in producing a book on educational methodology for graduate students are somewhat different from those for producing a high school chemistry book. Our discussion here of the production process, therefore, is highly simplified. You will receive frequent instructions from your editor on handling proofs, preparing an index, writing front matter, and so on, as your book goes through the production process.

Time Required for Production

After you have finished your writing and have shipped off the last installment to the sponsoring editor, you probably will begin to wonder how soon you will see finished books. The length of time required to produce a book varies from a few months to well over a year, depending on the size and complexity of your book, the additional work required on the manuscript, the number and type of illustrations, the workload of compositors and printers, the speed with which proof is processed, makeup problems, and so on. Hardly any publisher owns his own printing equipment (he contracts with printing and binding firms), and often he has little control over the manufacturers' scheduling problems. Remember that the publisher is just as anxious as you are to get your book on the market.

Many editing and production activities take place in order to produce a book. They do not always take place in the sequence described here.

Preliminary Examination

When your manuscript arrives on the sponsor's desk, it is examined carefully for organization, style problems, design elements, illustration opportunities, and so on. After the sponsor has satisfied himself that your manuscript is ready to be released for production, several conferences are held in which the production manager, designer, editing supervisor, illustrator, and others are present. At these meetings, basic decisions are made concerning costs, method of composition and printing, type of binding or packaging, size, art, color, schedules, and other matters, and the manuscript is turned over to the editing supervisor.

Copy Editing and Design

The supervisor reads the manuscript through carefully, noting any problems of organization or content and determining the style to be used in editing (see page

2). You will be asked to review his style recommendations, and you will also be consulted if, in the opinion of the supervisor, serious alterations are desired. Then the manuscript is styled: language problems are straightened out, and consistency in abbreviations, use of numbers, capitalization, spelling, and so on, is established. At the same time that this work is going on, the designer and illustrator are dealing with the problems of format, art, makeup, and the like.

Sample Pages

Once the designer has a clear picture of your book and decides on a basic design for it, he usually arranges to have portions of the manuscript set in type to see how the final product is going to look. These sample pages are discussed by the designer in conference with the editor and others. When there is agreement on the basic design, the sample pages will be sent to you for your inspection.

Keep in mind that the material in the sample pages may not run in the same sequence as your text content. It is often set from "bits and pieces"—perhaps several chapters apart—to get a visual impression of every separate design element in the manuscript.

When the design of the book is established, the manuscript is marked for type. Finally, with art, editing, and design work completed, the manuscript is sent to the typesetter (compositor).

Galley Proof

The typesetter first sets the manuscript in galleys. (A galley is a long tray that holds enough lines of type to make about $2\frac{1}{2}$ pages of an average book.)

Galley proofs contain no illustrations (except tables that can be set in type). Footnotes appear directly below the references to them in the text; headings may not be properly spaced; the paper is not of the grade that will be used in your book; the lines of type may be uneven or smudged. Don't let these things worry you; galleys have only a slight resemblance to the finished book.

Read Galleys Carefully

Galley proofs will be sent to you in installments, often directly from the compositor. Even though the printer's proofreader has read your galley proofs and checked them against the edited manuscript, you should read them *very carefully* yourself. The author's special technical competence puts him in a position to discover errors that a lay proofreader would not detect.

You will speed the production process along if you return each batch of galleys promptly, answering all queries that appear on the proof. The compositor can be making up pages of the first part of your book while the later parts are still being set in type.

Correcting Galley Proofs

Use proofreaders' marks in correcting galleys (see Figure 11); this will speed both the editing supervisor's and the printer's work.

The way in which you correct proof is different from the way you correct manuscript copy. On manuscript copy, you make changes above the line at the point of correction; on proof, you make changes in the margins (see Figure 12).

When correcting proof, use ink or pencil of a different color from the marks already on the proof. Put your marks in the right or left margin, whichever is nearer to the part corrected.

Figure 11. *Proofreaders' marks.*

Delete	lowercase Word
Delete and close up	Capital letter
Quad (one em) space	SMALL CAPITAL LETTER
Move down	Boldface type
Move up	Italic type
Move to left	Roman type
Move to right	Wrong font
Equalize spacing between words	Insert space
Broken letter	Close up
Begin a new paragraph	Turn letter
No new paragraph	Period
Let type stand as set	Comma
Verify or supply information	Apostrophe
Transpose letters or marked words	Quotation marks
Spell out (abbrev.) or (7)	Semicolon
Push space down	Colon
Straighten type	Question mark
Align type	Exclamation mark
Run in material on same line	Hyphen
Change (x/y) to built-up fraction	En dash
Change x/y to shilling fraction	Em dash
Set S as subscript	Two-em dash
Set S as exponent	Parentheses
	Brackets

Monotype Composition Co. | Check over carefully. Mark any corrections or changes legibly in margin of proof. | READD BY _Eth_
AUTHOR'S PROOF | | OK'd BY _une_

Galley 99 McGraw-Hill
NEUMANN—European Government—7020

refused to allow him to dominate it. The only visible difference between the Christian Democratic movement and the MRP was the attitude on Algeria, in which Bidault embraced the views of the Algerian ultras. But the attempt to replace the MRP failed.

In the elections of 1958, the MRP and Christian Democrats moved separately. Although many people supported the latter, they did so largely because of strong personal ties, dating back to the Resistance period, rather than because of sharing Bidault's views or ambitions. Although he was reelected by a wide margin in his own sixth district of the Loire department, he carried only twelve other Christian Democrats with him, while the MRP elected forty-four.

Bidault went into embittered retirement. He became an ever more violent apostle of the ultras in Algeria, made common cause with the army rebels, and went into voluntary though doubtless well-advised exile in South America.

It was quite important for France that the MRP had joined the first De Gaulle government as an act of national union, and that Pierre Pflimlin, the last Premier of the Fourth Republic, had entered De Gaulle's cabinet. Yet Robert Schuman watched developments from the sidelines, being well aware of General de Gaulle's hostility to European integration. And it was this hostility which on March 16, 1962, caused the resignation of all five MRP ministers in protest over the general's sharp and haughty rejection of European integration.

In opposition, the MRP concentrated primarily on two goals: one was the continued and vigorous advocacy of European unification, the other was the creation of a broad center-left movement. The party had already considerably rejuvenated itself by placing Jean Lecanuet in its presidency and electing Joseph Fontanet as secretary-general, both comparatively young men. At the same time the MRP leaders refused to accept the systematic anti-Gaullism of the Socialists and declared that they would vote for or against government propositions on their merits. This balanced attitude was rendered increasingly difficult by the crescendo of General de Gaulle's fight against European integration, and the brusque manner in which he publicly rejected Great Britain's entry into the European Common Market in January, 1963.

Thus, as the 1965 presidential elections approached, the MRP had generally moved from selective opposition to total opposition with the exception of a few veteran Gaullists like Maurice Schumann. It quietly supported the endeavor of Gaston Defferre for a broad center-left federation. After the failure of that experiment, the MRP leaders kept their own counsel and it was only quite late in the campaign that their president, Jean Lecanuet, presented his candidacy.[27]

[27] In order to emphasize his appeal to a segment of the population broader than just MRP voters, Lecanuet resigned as president of the MRP.

The Lecanuet candidacy had an electrifying effect, as discussed earlier. Although he had been a deputy in the Senate as well as a minor cabinet official, he was virtually unknown in France. Now he not only achieved great prominence but

Figure 12. How to mark galley and page proofs. This is part of a galley proof. Notice that the footnote has been placed at the point of reference. The query stamp alerts the author to a copy editor's question on a corresponding page of the manuscript. The author crosses out proof queries to show that he has seen them.

Page Proof

After galley proof has been returned to the compositor and he has made the necessary corrections, the galleys are broken into page lengths. The page proofs you will receive usually show the illustrations in the proper position (with accompanying legends), page numbers, running heads, and so on.

Page proofs will be read with care by our own proofreaders, but it is imperative for you to read them carefully too—this is your last chance to eliminate errors. Also check illustrations and their legends (to the layman's eyes some complicated drawings and photographs look "correct" when they are upside down!). But make only *necessary* changes at this stage; corrections in page proof are very costly.

Cost of Corrections on Proof

Upon receiving proof, some authors suddenly decide to rewrite the book. Of course, if there are errors of fact or outdated materials, corrections must be made. But this is not the time to worry about the finer points of writing—polishing your writing at this stage can cost you money, and it will undoubtedly delay publication of the book.

The costs of corrections always mount up much more rapidly than the inexperienced author expects. The original typesetting is done by machine. Corrections require hand work, and minor corrections often result in the resetting of considerable material. The charge for altering 20 percent of the lines in a galley proof will amount to a good deal more than 20 percent of the original composition cost. And corrections made in page proof cost much more than those made in galley proof.

You should therefore try to "justify" (compensate for) your corrections by adding the same number of letters that you delete or by striking out a word or words to make room for an addition.

The accompanying example shows the amount of resetting necessitated by the *uncompensated* addition of a single word in page proof. Here is the page proof corrected by the author. He indicates that he wants to insert the word *alternately* on the third line, but fails to delete a comparable number of characters.

When the coil is energized, the armature is attracted, and upon its release it vibrates with unvarying frequency but with gradual damping. The associated springs are adjusted ˄to receive intermittent contact until, as the damping progresses, the amplitude of vibration decreases below the point of contact. Associated slow-release relays are held energized by the intermittent impulses of current allowed to flow by the rapid succession of contacts thus made and, of course, are released when the vibration dies down to a point where the contacts are no longer made. Since

alternately /

the frequency of the reed vibration is constant and its damping a governable quantity, the time periods determined by the adjustment of the springs can be made of such length as to be measured in seconds rather than in fractions of a second, as in the ordinary slow-release relays.

Here is the proof after resetting. Notice that twelve lines had to be reset in order to add one word without a comparable deletion.

When the coil is energized, the armature is attracted, and upon its release it vibrates with unvarying frequency but with gradual damping. The associated springs are adjusted alternately to receive intermittent contact until, as the damping progresses, the amplitude of vibration decreases below the point of contact. Associated slow-release relays are held energized by the intermittent impulses of current allowed to flow by the rapid succession of contacts thus made and, of course, are released when the vibration dies down to a point where the contacts are no longer made. Since the frequency of the reed vibration is constant and its damping a governable quantity, the time periods determined by the adjustment of the springs can be made of such length as to be measured in seconds rather than in fractions of a second, as in the ordinary slow-release relays.

Heavy resetting in page proof also leads to the risk of introducing new typographical errors, dropping lines of type, or requiring unexpected alterations in page makeup.

HOW
TO
PREPARE
THE
INDEX

HOW TO PREPARE THE INDEX

The Value of a Good Index

People often judge a book by its index. If the index directs the reader quickly to the item he is looking for, he pronounces the book useful. If it does not, the reader's attitude toward the volume may be negative no matter how good the content is.

The main purpose of an index is to make a textbook, reference book, or handbook more useful. A good index also has many possibilities as a sales feature. Reviewers, casual browsers, and teachers often turn to the index first to get the "feel" of a book. A person considering purchasing the book or adopting it for class use often wonders how a particular subject is handled and immediately goes to the index to find out where the topic is covered.

Most books have a single index containing subjects, place names, and personal names in one alphabetical sequence because this is more convenient for readers. Sometimes, if there are more than a hundred personal names, a separate name index is used. If you are not sure whether your book would be more useful with a name index, ask your editor.

Who Should Make the Index

Who should make the index for a book? There is little doubt that the person best qualified for the job is the author himself. He has labored mightily to write the book and knows exactly what its major topics are, what people are likely to look for in the way of information, and the nuances of reference that are likely to escape the uninitiated.

Some authors make excellent indexes and enjoy doing it; others are bored or baffled by what seems to be a tedious and difficult job. The index has to be prepared in the final stages of publication when the author often has other commitments. If you don't have the time or the inclination to prepare the index, you should engage an experienced, competent indexer. Or you may ask McGraw-Hill to have one of its on-call free-lance indexers do the job. Remember, though, that the index is the author's responsibility, and the cost of preparing it must be borne by him. When we have the index done for you, we pay the indexer and charge the cost against your future royalties; the amount charged by the indexer depends, of course, on the length of the index and the complexity of the job.

When the Index Should Be Prepared

The final index cannot be prepared until page proof of the book is received by the author. However, some authors begin to organize the index and select the items when galley proof is completed. Although they can't indicate page numbers at this point, they can take some of the pressure off the final preparation when everything seems to be due at once.

At the latest, the author should begin to prepare his index as soon as the first installment of page proof arrives. The complete index should be in the publisher's hands within ten days after the last batch of page proof is received.

What Should Be Indexed

Indexing must be selective. An indexer who tries to include every possible reference to a subject will find himself accumulating a solid block of page numbers, every one of which the reader will have to look up before he can tell whether the subject is fully discussed or merely mentioned. No doubt you have found indexes with this fault or with some others that you want to avoid. It may be a good idea to study the indexes of several books in your field of interest and to use some of the best ones as models.

If you look at an actual index, or at the sample index shown in Figure 15, you will see the difference between main entries and subentries. A subentry shows what aspect or division of a subject is found on certain pages. Use subentries freely, and make them as specific as possible.

Don't try to index a subject in every form under which a reader might look for it. In any field of knowledge there are synonymous terms; you know them and your readers will probably know them. For example, in a medical book the entries under *heart disease* should not be duplicated (or partly duplicated) under *cardiac disease*. In a book on architecture *classic revival* and *Greek revival* are synonyms. Choose one form, put all relevant information there, and make *see* references from other possible forms.

In selecting items to be indexed, include maps, tables, and illustrations. List them under their subjects and identify them in some such way as this:

Alloys, properties, table
California, forests, map
Printed circuits, plating, illus.

The identifying word or abbreviation may be italicized for emphasis.

Certain items are not usually indexed, although they may be if you feel they are particularly important for your book. Among these are:

1. Bibliographies, problems, and similar features appearing at the end of every chapter
2. Separate items in tables
3. Parts of maps or illustrations

Bibliographic footnotes may or may not be indexed. This depends partly on the character of the book, and you can decide whether you want to include them. If you do, you will probably need a separate name index.

Choosing the Entries

As you *reread* your page proof for the purposes of indexing (don't try to read proof for errors and prepare the index at the same time—each operation requires your undivided attention), think about the principal ideas that appear on each page. You may underline these main ideas on your proof as you read.

In selecting your entries, beware of subjects that are very broad. For example, the index to a book on monetary policy should not be dominated by the term *Monetary policy*. A history of the United States may not have any index entries under *United States, history*. Even chapter and section or unit titles are not used as index entries unless they contain key words that the reader would ordinarily look for. However, they can help to provide the basic framework for your index because presumably they represent the major ideas in your book.

When choosing the references a reader might want to look up, think carefully about where he will expect to find them—that is, the key word he will seek. For example, the person who wants to know something about the history of Chinese pottery would not look under the word *History*. Rather, he would look under *Chinese pottery* or *Pottery, Chinese*. The key words here, then, are *Chinese* and *pottery*.

Making the Index

Every entry and subentry for the index should be on a separate card for convenience in alphabetizing.

If you are working with an assistant who will type the index cards from marked page proof, you can devise a system of marking to show whether a word is to be used as a main entry or a subentry. If the exact words you want are not in the text, they can be written in the margin. If you are preparing your own index cards, the marks on the proof are for your convenience only; use them if you find them helpful. Some professional indexers never mark proof at all.

Preparation of Cards

Regular 3 by 5 cards are convenient, and fairly substantial cards are easier to handle than flimsy scratch paper.

Every card must have a main entry. Notice this in Figure 13. Without the main entry it would be impossible to tell where the subentry belonged.

Subentries and Sub-subentries. In the printed index each subentry will be on a separate line, indented from the main entry to which it refers. Sometimes a second value of subentry is needed, indented from the preceding first-value subentry. The sample index (Figure 15) shows how this is done. Try to avoid using more than two values of subentries. The effect of complicated indentions in narrow columns is unsightly and confusing. If you use a sub-subentry, the main entry and the subentry to which it is related must be on the same card.

Form of Entries

In every index entry or subentry the most significant word should come first. This is necessary because an index is in alphabetical order for the convenience of readers. Sometimes the significant word is obvious to the indexer, as it will be to the reader, but often the choice of this word requires imagination and judgment. For example, *Hints on repairing ac-dc motors* is not a suitable index entry because nobody would look for the word "hints." Should the subject be listed as *Ac-dc motors, repairs,* or as *Repairs, ac-dc motors,* or in both forms? That depends on the subject matter of the book and the general plan of the index.

Prepositions may be used in subentries to show how the subjects are related to the main entry, or they may be omitted if the meaning is clear without them. In the preceding paragraph, *repairs of* would be no clearer than *repairs.*

Two Key Words. When an entry contains two key words, either of which might be looked for in the index, make two cards. For example, in the illustration of Chinese pottery, make one card for *Chinese pottery* and another for *Pottery, Chinese.* Be sure that the same page numbers appear on both cards. If the subject of Chinese pottery is discussed elsewhere under another title, such as *ceramics,* include that page also, to keep all relevant information together.

Adjectives in Entries. An entry should be a noun or a substantive phrase. An adjective should not be used alone, such as:

> Adult:
> education
> medical care
> travel preferences

It may, however, be the leading word in a key phrase if it is more likely to be looked up than the noun that follows it. For example:

> Adult education:
> growth of
> methods of instruction
> trends in

The adjective must be repeated in each entry on the cards: *Adult education, Adult institutions, Adult organizations.*

Simplifying Wording. Sometimes the exact wording of the text may be too complex or cumbersome for an entry or subentry, and you must then find a simpler way to write it. For instance, if you select *Accidents* as an index entry, do not in the subentry quote from the text, "how to keep them from happening" or "what to do in case of." Your subentries in the index should be *prevention of* and *first aid in.*

Footnotes. Footnotes are not usually indexed unless they contain information which is not in the text. When they are indexed they appear as follows:

Reports:
business, 14, 487–494
parts of, 494–496
titles, 268n

In the last subentry, "titles, 268n," the n refers to the footnote. If a text reference and its footnote reference are on the same page, list the page only once without n.

Page Numbers.   Be sure that page numbers are accurate; check and double-check them. Page numbers should be given in full: *178–182*, not *178–82*. Avoid the use of *ff.* or *et seq.* You may use inclusive page numbers for three or more consecutive pages, even if the discussion is not continuous.

Cross References.   Cross references in an index direct the reader to related subjects. Two types of cross reference are used, *see* and *See also*. A *see* reference directs the reader from a term given without page numbers to the entry where they are listed. If an entry appears in two forms (*Diesel engines* and *Engines, diesel*), it may be possible to give all necessary page numbers in both places. But if the entry is long, with many page numbers or subentries, one form should be selected and the other should be made a *see* reference.

Engines, diesel (*see* Diesel engines)

A *See also* reference shows where additional information can be found. If the book gives detailed descriptions of several types of engines, the entry *Engines* may be used for the subject as a whole with subentries referring to general discussions of history, inventions, and theories. After the last subentry a cross reference to specific types of engines may read:

(*See also* Diesel engines; Jet engines; Steam engines)

See also should not be used to call attention to the same page numbers, or perhaps different ones, under another form of the same entry.

Names of Persons.   Names of persons in the index are given in full; that is, the surname is followed by a given name or initials, even though the full name may not appear in the text. Identical surnames are repeated.

This	*But not this*
Burton, Arnold S.	Burton, Arnold S.
Burton, Melvin Rath	" , Melvin Rath

Alphabetizing

Some indexers wait until all cards are made before alphabetizing them. It is much easier to prepare a well-organized and consistent index if you alphabetize the cards as soon as they are made. In this way you can see the structure of the index as a whole and solve your problems as you find them.

You will save time too. If you find a second reference to a subject you have used before, just add another page number to the card. If you find too many page numbers accumulating, think of subentries that can be used to divide them. It is much easier to do this in the early stages of an index than to wait until the last minute and discover that you have ten cards for the same subject.

Alphabetizing is not as easy as it looks, and several problems are likely to occur. The following standard rules are helpful.

1. Alphabetize word by word, so that a short word comes before a long one beginning with the same letters. Thus *radio, radio broadcasting,* and *radio stations* go together before *radioactivity.* In chemical indexes, where names of compounds may or may not be hyphenated, alphabetizing is sometimes letter by letter, ignoring the division of words, but the separate-word style is better for most subjects.

2. Disregard prepositions and conjunctions in alphabetizing, whether they appear within entries or at the beginning of subentries. *Society of Modern Management* goes before *Society for Professional Advancement,* and *of France* precedes *in Great Britain* as a subentry. A possible exception is in books on art and literature where titles are indexed. *The Man on the Flying Trapeze* should precede *The Man without a Country.*

3. A proper noun precedes a common noun of the same spelling: the name *Battles, Sir William F.* comes before the common noun *battles.*

4. The name of a person precedes the name of a place: *Washington, George* comes before *Washington, D.C.*

5. Names beginning with *Mc* are alphabetized as if they were spelled *Mac.*

6. A surname followed by initials is alphabetized before one with a spelled-out name: *Rogers, R. K.* comes before *Rogers, Raymond.*

7. Titles like *Sir, Gen.,* and *Dr.* are ignored in alphabetizing names.

8. Numbers are usually alphabetized as if they were spelled out: *1000* is alphabetized as *one thousand,* and *1984* as *nineteen-eighty-four.* Sometimes, however, numbers are arranged in numerical sequence, especially when they follow names or when they appear in subentries:

Census:	Henry V
1790	Henry VI
1880	Henry VII
1960	Henry VIII

9. Some common abbreviations, especially in geographical names, are hardly ever spelled out, but they are alphabetized as if they were. *Mt. Vernon* goes before *mountains; St. Louis* before *San Francisco. U.S.S.R.* (Union of Soviet Socialist Republics) goes before *U.S.* (United States).

10. Abbreviations are often more familiar than the words they represent, and some, such as *Rh factor* and *pH,* have no exact spelled-out equivalents. In a book on labor relations AFL-CIO might be more familiar as well as more convenient than the spelled-out form. Aside from the ex-

ceptions described in paragraph 9, abbreviations are alphabetized according to the sequence of letters as if they were words. It is often advisable to make a cross reference from the spelled-out form:

Dichlorodiphenyltrichloroethane (*see* DDT)

When the spelled-out form is used as an entry, the abbreviation can be given after it in parentheses.

11. Words with hyphenated prefixes are treated as solid words: *Panama* goes before *Pan-American*. But hyphenated combinations of words such as *right-to-left shunt* are alphabetized as separate words.

12. In alphabetizing chemical terms, prefixed symbols and numbers are disregarded. Thus *d-fructose* is alphabetized as *fructose* and *17-ketosteroids* as *ketosteroids*. For capitalization, too, the prefixes are disregarded: *d-Fructose, 17-Ketosteroids*.

Editing the Cards

Even if you have kept all your cards in alphabetical order and planned the structure and relationship of entries carefully, the final editing is important. Now you can see the index as a whole. Is there any needless repetition? Have you any synonymous terms such as *Atomic power* and *Nuclear power* that can be combined? Have you ever used both singular and plural forms such as *Artery* and *Arteries*? If you have used two forms of the same entry, such as *Consumer cooperatives* and *Cooperatives, consumer*, are the same page numbers in both places?

Verify all cross references—nothing is more irritating to a reader than being told to *see* or *See also* an entry that does not exist. Has this ever happened to you?

Notice the punctuation and capitalization of entries as shown in the examples we have given. Copy for your index should be in the same style, as follows:

1. The first word of a main entry is capitalized, as are all words normally capitalized in the text. The first word of a subentry is lowercase unless it is capitalized in the text.

2. A main entry or subentry is followed by a comma before the first page number. Page numbers are separated by commas.

3. When a main entry is not followed by page numbers, it stands on a separate line, followed by a colon. The first subentry appears on the next line.

Cooperatives:
    agricultural marketing, 621–626
    consumer, 630–637

4. If a subentry has no page numbers but is followed by secondary sub-entries, this form is used:

> Agricultural marketing:
>   market structure: changes in, 613–616
>   traditional, 610–613

Check Alphabetization Carefully.   This should be done as a separate opera-tion, the last step in handling the cards. Then there will be no chance of moving cards around and misfiling them.

Marking Cards for Typing

Marking is a simple mechanical operation. It can be done while you are editing and revising the cards. If you find this too confusing, you can mark the cards later, but then they will have to be handled twice. Only two kinds of marking are needed.

1. On cards for subentries, cross out main entries that are not to be printed. If a card is for a second-value subentry, cross out both the main entry and the first subentry. Even if you are typing your own index, you will do it better with these markings.
2. Indicate the indention of subentries. A subentry of the first value is pre-ceded by ☐ , a printer's symbol meaning "indent one em." A second-value subentry is preceded by ☐☐ ("indent two ems"). The marked cards will look like the sample in Figure 13.

Typing the Index Manuscript

Typing is the last step in the preparation of an index. Typed copy should be on 8½ by 11 paper, double-spaced, and in a single column. Show indention of sub-entries by using two typewriter spaces for each step marked ☐ on the cards. Turnover lines (subsequent lines of entries too long to fit on one line) should be indented five spaces or more so that they will not be mistaken for subentries. Send the original and one carbon copy of your typed index to your editor.

A portion of a typewritten index is shown in Figure 14.

A printed index is illustrated in Figure 15 with marginal comments on form and style.

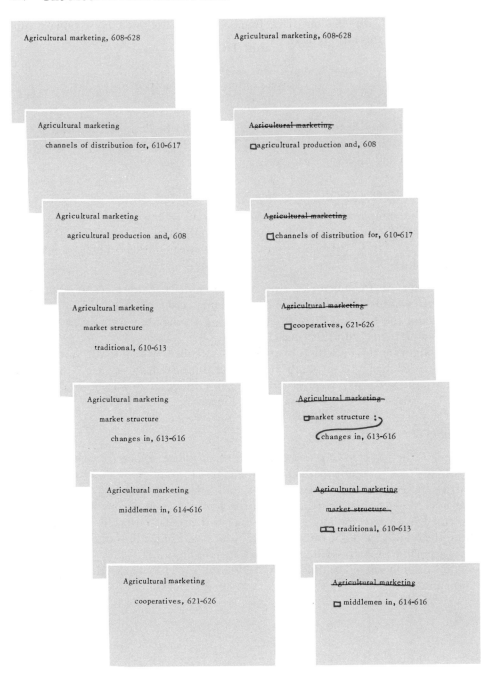

Figure 13. *Left, typed index cards; right, the same cards alphabetized and marked for final typing of the index manuscript.*

```
AFL-CIO, 36-48, 192

    arbitration, 114-120

    in automobile industry, 230-232

    history, 37-39

Agricultural marketing, 608-628

    agricultural production and, 608

    channels of distribution for, 610-
        617

    cooperatives, 621-626

    market structure: changes in,
        613-616

        traditional, 610-613

    middlemen in, 614-616
```

Figure 14.   Typed index manuscript.

Abbreviation alphabetized by letter sequence	AFL-CIO, 36–48, 192
	    arbitration, 114–120
	    in automobile industry,
	        230–232
	    history, 37–39
	Agricultural marketing, 608–
	    628

Subentries with turnover lines	agricultural production
	        and, 608
	    channels of distribution for,
	        610–617
	    cooperatives, 621–626

Sub-entries	market structure: changes in,
	        613–616
	        traditional, 610–613
	    middlemen in, 614–616
	Air conditioning, 423, 439–448

Prepositions ignored in alphabetizing	for comfort, 440
	    in factories, 335, 441–443
	    as incentive to work, 442
	Air pollution, 248, 486–501
	    in Cleveland, 308
	    in Pittsburgh, 332–334
	    studies, 489–496
	        Los Angeles, 487
	        New York, 493–495
	        Newark, 496

Alphabetize by solid words: "Aircraft" follows all entries beginning with "Air"	Aircraft design, 253, 267, 310
	Aircraft pilots, training, 256–
	    258
	Aluminum Corporation of America
	    (ALCOA), 248

Cross reference (see)	American Federation of Labor (*see* AFL-CIO)

Main entry without page numbers	Arbitration:
	    AFL-CIO, 114–120
	    compulsory, 124–131

Cross reference (See also)	(*See also* Mediation)

Figure 15. Sample index.

Automobile industry:
  AFL-CIO, 230–232
  wages, 318, 320

Space between A and B

Bell, Alexander Graham, 14
Bell, alarm, 287

Proper name before common noun

Bell-shaped curve in statistics, 29

*Compound adjective alpha-
betized as two words*

Bellingham, J. H., Inc.,
  436

Firm name, inverted position

Birth rate:
  increase in, 516–524
  1930, 521
  1945, 522
  2000, estimated, 523–524

Dates in sequence

Cleveland, Grover, 26
Cleveland:
  air pollution, 308
  traffic survey, 542

Personal name before place

Collective bargaining, 124–132
Collective-bargaining clause,
  126, 130

Adjective repeated after noun

Cooperatives:
  agricultural marketing, 621–
    626
  consumer, 630–637

*Main entries repeated here as
subentries*

Davis, D. R., 107
Davis, D. R., Jr., 138

Position of Jr.

Delacey, M. L., 96*n.*, 605

n. for footnote

De La Mare, F. C., 92

Compound name as solid word

Delaware Valley watershed,
  456–457
Do-it-yourself hobbies, equipment for, 556, 558

*Main entry with only one
subentry, run in*

Doctors (*see* Health services;
  Hospitalization; Medical care)

*Cross references in alphabetical
order*

PREPARING
A
REVISION

PREPARING A REVISION

Reprints versus Revisions

Reprints

When the inventory of the first printing is substantially reduced, a new printing must be ordered. (The publisher tries to anticipate the need for a new printing long before the first printing is exhausted.) You will receive notice that the book is to be reprinted—say, three months hence—and you will be asked to submit any corrections that should be made. At this point, only glaring deficiencies are corrected—printer's errors, inaccurate dates, misspellings, and so on. This is not the time to make extensive changes; you would hold up the new printing, and those who are waiting for stock might have to adopt another textbook. Therefore, save your major changes for a revision.

Revisions

The typical revision cycle for a textbook is every five years, but this is not a hard-and-fast rule. Some books may be revised in their second or third year of publication, depending on market conditions, competition, and changes in fact, philosophy, or technology that call for new content. Other successful books may not be revised until they have been on the market six, or even seven, years.

After your book is published, your editor watches its sales and keeps an eye on general market trends. Generally, he will know within two years after publication whether the book will be successful enough to warrant a new edition, and he will get in touch with you long before he needs your manuscript for the revision.

Extent of Revision

How extensive should your revision be? The answer to that question will, of course, vary greatly from one book to another. For some books, the subject matter changes very little from year to year, and often all that is required is an updating of current facts and perhaps minor reorganization based on recommendations made by users of the material. Other books require very heavy revision; major advances in the discipline or subject area, changes in teaching methods, or publication of competitive texts may force the author virtually to rewrite the book.

How extensive must a revision be in order to justify a new copyright? This question has been debated for years, but no definitive answer has been found. We feel that the new edition of a book should normally contain at least 25 percent new content in order to call it "new." But this is an arbitrary figure; besides, it is very difficult to decide what "25 percent new content" means. Does it mean that the author must change 25 words out of every 100? Suppose he reorganizes a chapter completely, to improve its flow and to make it easier to teach, but disturbs the actual content very little. How is this counted?

Let's put it this way: You must satisfy yourself that you have the best possible coverage of your subject, that all your facts and figures are up to date, and that you are not simply going back on the market with essentially the same book you originally published. Most subjects offer plenty of opportunity for presenting new data, introducing better organization, and improving the writing. At the same time, there is nearly always "deadwood" that can be replaced with fresh material.

You and your editor will usually have several face-to-face discussions about your revision. He will have recommendations to make, based on the feedback he has had from sales representatives and customers. In some cases, the editor will suggest that you develop a questionnaire to be sent to users of your book, asking them to react to the present treatment as well as to proposed ideas for a revision. Even though the critics of your book may disagree on its "plus" and "minus" features, you will nearly always receive a few good direction signals to guide you in a revision. The questionnaire may be sent to all users (the publisher keeps a record of those who have purchased the book for classroom use), or it may be sent to twenty or so selected institutions of various sizes and at different locations. Reactions may also be sought from McGraw-Hill consultants and advisers.

Time Allowed for Revision

Generally speaking, you will be given at least one year to do your revision. There are exceptions, of course. In unusual situations, market conditions may require that we ask you to have your revision completed in three or four months. Typically, though, we are interested in a more extensive revision than suggested by a hurry-up job. You and the editor may decide that you need fifteen to eighteen months in which to plan and write the revision your book needs.

When to Start

It's a good idea to assume that there *will be* a revision of your book and to begin to make preparation for it as early as possible. If you are the typical textbook author, you will set up a "revision" folder when you are in the last throes of completing the current edition. You start by filing the new ideas that came too late to be incorporated into the present volume. Then, as you keep up with your professional reading and research, attend conventions and conferences, talk with publishing representatives and editors, and correspond with your colleagues, you enter appropriate notes, clippings, booklets, etc., in the file. As your ideas expand, you will probably want to set up several folders, organized by the major topics of your current edition. Many authors keep a "revision copy" of their book in which they enter changes and corrections.

Procedure for Revision

Most revisions are reset; that is, new galleys of type are made. At one time, it was desirable to retain as much of the original composition as possible, in the interest of speed and economy. For some books, this is still true. But the costs and methods of printing today usually make it just as fast and economical to reset a book as to patch old composition and salvage the printing plates. At any rate, the editor and manufacturing manager in McGraw-Hill will study your revision plans and determine whether it is better to reset the new edition or try to patch your present book and avoid new composition. You will be given the instructions you need.

Materials

Here are the materials you will need in preparing your revision.

Paper. Use regular 8½ by 11 sheets of good manuscript paper (see page 20).

Unbound Sheets of Your Book. When you and the editor agree that a revision is to be undertaken, the editor will send you two or more copies of your present book in loose sheets. If corrections are minor, these pages, or parts of them, may be pasted up on 8½ by 11 paper to avoid retyping. If your revision is to be very heavy, you may not want to make use of these sheets, preferring to submit completely new typewritten copy. In most cases, however, a considerable amount of material from the current book can be used almost intact, and there is no point in your retyping these pages when the changes in them are minor. The text sheets supplied by the editor will have been taken from the latest printing. (Don't use page proof left over from the previous edition.)

Rubber Cement. Use rubber cement to mount your text sheets on the manuscript paper. Please don't use staples, pins, clips, cellophane tape, or library paste.

Pen and Ink. Use ink (blue or black) and a fine-pointed pen for notes and corrections.

Mounting the Unbound Sheets

Whole Pages. Center the pages on one side of your manuscript paper, using one set of sheets for left-hand pages, one for right. Apply rubber cement over the entire surface, not in dabs at corners.

Pamphlets and Other Publications. Don't submit bound pamphlets or other materials as part of the manuscript. Mount printed material to be quoted just as you mount reprint copy of your own book, using two sets of sheets.

Parts of Pages. Cut and mount parts of pages in proper sequence with new typed material, or mount on separate pages. If you are picking up less than half a page of several small patches from scattered paragraphs, it is better to retype this material.

Margins.   Whether the pages contain only new copy or a combination of re-print copy and new copy, allow margins of at least 1½ inches all around.

Double-column Material.   Cut apart double-column material, and paste each column on a separate sheet, centered.

Discarded Material.   Don't bother to mount blank pages or sheets consisting entirely of text or illustrations that are not to be used.

Making Corrections

Make whatever changes you feel are desirable in the mounted unbound sheets. Unless it is agreed that the revision will be minor and the plates will be patched, don't hold back on your changes to save composition for the sake of economy.

Minor Alterations.   You may make minor alterations directly on the un-bound sheets (see Figure 16). Write legibly in ink, or if the correction is more than eight or ten words long, type with double spacing. If possible, type all *mathematical material.* Write inserts horizontally (never vertically) in the margin, as though you were correcting proof. Use a caret within the text line to show where the change is to be made. Please don't superimpose your correc-tions on the printed material, although you may write directly above the line if there is enough space between lines to make the alteration clearly legible.

Cross out with a heavy line any material to be deleted. A felt-tip pen is excellent for this purpose.

Major Alterations.   When corrections begin to clutter the page (often after four or five big ones), it is best to retype the material. Printers charge a pen-alty for copy that is hard to read and that slows down composition. In making long inserts, we would rather you cut the unbound book sheet apart and insert the typewritten addition in its proper sequence.

Styling of New and Old Material

New material should ordinarily match the old in abbreviations, spelling, capital-ization, etc.; however, tell us about outmoded usages you are aware of, and the editing supervisor will check them out. On request, we can send you a copy of the style sheet prepared for the previous edition, and you may note on it or list separately any detailed changes you want made.

Numbering

Check the numbering of figures, paragraphs, equations, and tables and all cross references to them. Indicate necessary changes in the numbering of tables, both in the table title and in the text. Page numbers referred to in the text should be crossed out and the notation "00" indicated in the margin.

Cross references to illustrations should not be changed until all illustra-tions have been obtained and permission secured.

182

third party would, to the extent of the waiver, defeat the subrogation right of the insurer and would relieve the insurer of payment of loss to the same extent. Some insurers go so far as to insert a clause in the contract making it void in the event of such waiver. But insurance contracts are adapted to the realities of customary release or reduction of liability by agreement between the insured and the bailee.

who is responsible in considerable measure for the safety of the property.

If there is a conflict between the insurance contract and the contract between the insured and the bailee, use is made of a *loan receipt*. Under the terms of this receipt the insurer lends the amount of the loss under the insurance to the insured, but does not pay the loss as such. It then makes claim against the bailee in the name of the insured, and if necessary sues in his name to enforce the claim. To the extent that recovery is had against the bailee, the loan is repaid; any part of the loan not so covered is forgiven.

If

Loss of Parts. In case of a loss of a part of a set or of other property, *is lost,* it might be claimed that, because the remainder was valueless or of less than its proportionate value, the insurer would be liable for a total or disproportionate loss. Inland-marine contracts frequently contain clauses designed to limit the insurer's liability to a fair proportion of the total value of the set or to the value of the particular part of other property lost. For example, the loss of one cuff link of a pair valued at $100 would call for payment of $50. Similarly, loss to labels, capsules, or wrappers is limited to the amount sufficient to pay the cost of new ones and to recondition the goods involved in the loss.

Interpretation of the Contract. Should the inland-marine contract be interpreted in accordance with the rules applicable to marine-insurance contracts or those applicable to fire and casualty contracts? This question has arisen from time to time. The tendency seems to be to apply fire and casualty general rules, which are more favorable to the insured.

The Contracts. No attempt will be made here to explain, or even to list, all inland-marine contracts. A few outstanding examples will be discussed as an indication of the sort of risk that may be covered by such contracts. It is intended to put the reader on notice of the kind of property or situation that should suggest inquiry into the possibilities of inland marine insurance. Lack of standardization and

12

For an extensive discussion of bailee risks, see Prentiss B. Reed, "Adjustment of Property Losses," chap. 16.

Figure 16.   Alterations in mounted sheet.

Illustrations

If illustrations from the present edition are to be reused in the revision, find out from your editor whether the old printing plates can be salvaged or whether it will be necessary to supply the original drawings and photographs. New illustrations should be handled in accordance with the instructions given on pages 28 to 31.

Renumber illustration copy in proper sequence, and make a working list of old and new figure numbers for your convenience and ours.

Legends. Number the legends (captions) for both old and new illustrations to match the new numbers on the illustration copy. Retype the legend list in duplicate, double-spaced.

Obsolete Material. When updating is desirable, discard old pictures that portray out-of-date clothing styles, equipment, etc., even though the main object in the illustration may not be in disuse.

Permissions

Obtain all necessary permissions for new illustrations, text, and tables from the original copyright holders.

Front Matter

Submit the following items with the revised manuscript:

1. A new table of contents
2. A new preface that calls attention to the significant changes and incorporates whatever is appropriate of the text of previous prefaces
3. A title page with up-to-date affiliations of all authors
4. Any other items such as frontispiece, dedication, or introduction, whether or not these are to be changed

Final Reading

After all material has been assembled, number the pages of the text in sequence, disregarding old page numbers. Then reread the entire manuscript to catch errors in fact, out-of-date or vague allusions to events and persons (*after the war, the President* . . .), such expressions as *at present* and *during the past decade,* and references to bibliographic material no longer pertinent or available.

Again check continuity, sequence of numbered items, cross references, and correlation of text with illustrations.

Index

If the text has been reset, you must prepare a new index from page proof (just as you would for a new book). Even though you may use the old index as the basis for preparing the new one, we should receive only the new copy, typed single-column, double-spaced. Be sure to check the form and page numbers of all entries; it is easy to overlook a few original references when working from reprint copy.

If the text has not been reset and very few changes in page numbers or additional entries are required, the index from the previous edition is acceptable. Mount each column on a separate sheet, and add or correct copy neatly in the margins. Be sure to eliminate entries that refer to material that has been deleted.

HOW
WE
MARKET
YOUR
BOOK

HOW WE MARKET YOUR BOOK

Those responsible for promoting and selling McGraw-Hill books are brought into a discussion of it long before the contract is sent to the author for signature. When the project first comes to the attention of the editor, he meets with the marketing director in his division to discuss the sales potential of the book. Conferences are also held with other sales people who specialize in various markets. Let's say, for example, that the book is on personnel supervision and its primary market is in colleges and universities. The college sponsoring editor will talk to those who market books to business, government, and professional people by mail and through bookstores; to others who specialize in technical school and terminal college markets; to others who sell books to countries throughout the world; and so on. This "across-the-board" policy of McGraw-Hill ensures the widest possible distribution of your book.

As soon as the manuscript is far enough along to estimate a publication date, the various divisions that intend to sell it in their particular markets begin to plan their selling and promotion efforts. As the writing proceeds and the author and editor exchange communications about the project, the editor feeds information about the book's features to the marketing people. In turn, he frequently receives suggestions that might enhance the appeal of the book, and these suggestions are passed along to the author.

When the publication date is fairly certain, the advertising and sales promotion people move into action. Although they have received from the editor complete information about the book, they will also want the author's assistance. You will be asked to complete a marketing questionnaire, which calls for information on the principal features of your book, the audience for which it is intended, how the book differs from and is superior to competing texts, periodicals to which you believe copies should be sent for review, suggestions on how the book might best be advertised and promoted, special lists of people likely to be interested in the book, and so on.

Preparation also begins at this time for listing the book in our general and specialized catalogs; for advertising in journals, newspapers, and magazines; and for designing and producing letters and circulars to be sent to potential customers.

Several months before publication, travelers and other sales personnel discuss the forthcoming book with their customers and begin sending in to the marketing directors names of people who should receive examination or review copies and of others who can be influential in establishing the market for the book.

When the book is finally published, copies are sent immediately to those recommended by the salesmen as well as others who have expressed interest in seeing the book. Salesmen call on teachers and professors, department heads, supervisors, and administrators in schools and colleges; on book jobbers or

Stephen M. Zollo
Sponsoring Editor
Gregg Division; 29th floor
McGraw-Hill Book Company
1221 Avenue of the Americas
New York, NY 10020

dealers; and on librarians. They make presentations before textbook committees and "work" state adoptions (if the book is an elementary or high-school text).

Intensive selling—both direct and indirect—continues throughout the life of your book. Follow-up advertising at key selling times keeps it in the public eye, stressing particularly those qualities, uses, and features which experience has shown to be major selling points. The author is continually advised of our sales efforts—promotion material distributed, advertising, important adoptions, and so on.

We invite the author to react to our sales and promotion activities in behalf of his book. We also welcome his suggestions about conventions where the book may be exhibited, curriculum developments that may open new sales avenues, information about changes in personnel that may have a bearing on the adoption of his book, and information he may have on competitive situations.

THIS
IS
McGRAW-HILL

THIS IS McGRAW-HILL

McGraw-Hill is a general diversified publisher and producer of books, encyclopedias, handbooks, reference books, workbooks, paperbacks, manuals, guides, programs, films, filmstrips, film loops, transparencies, records, tapes, tests, science kits, and instructional systems and equipment.

We publish in the fields of physical, biological, behavioral, and social sciences; fiction, religion, biography, art, and general nonfiction; the humanities, foreign languages, and language arts; law, architecture, engineering, technical education, vocational and industrial arts, and business education; medicine, dentistry, nursing, and the health professions. And we produce schoolbooks, story books, and picture books for children.

We publish in the United States and abroad, and reach around the world through our own multilanguage editions and through the further sales of foreign rights in more than fifty languages.

The operating divisions and subsidiary units of the Book Company are as follows.

Elementary and High School

Webster Division

Serves the preschool through twelfth grades with a full range of books, films, and other types of educational materials and equipment. Publishes special materials for in-school remedial programs and adult basic education courses.

California Test Bureau

Publishes standardized intelligence, aptitude, and achievement tests, principally for the school market, but for colleges and industry as well.

Gregg Division

Publishes for office, business, and distributive education at the high school and post-high school levels. The leading business education publisher in the country.

Higher Education and Professional

College Division

Serves all disciplines at the collegiate level, undergraduate and graduate. Ranked as a leading, or perhaps *the* leading, college publisher in the United States.

Technical and Vocational Education Division

Publishes for post-high school and technical institute markets, as well as for high school industrial and vocational arts programs.

Capitol Radio Engineering Institute, Inc. (a subsidiary)

Offers self-study programs in electronics and nuclear technology. CREI is fully accredited by the National Home Study Council and enrolls more than 30,000 students.

Blakiston Division

Publishes professional and academic texts and reference works in medicine, dentistry, nursing, and the health occupations.

Industrial and Business Books Division

Publishes for the professional, business, industrial, engineering, and management markets.

Legal Publications

Publishes general and reference works in law.

Shepard's Citations, Inc. (a subsidiary)

Publishes citations, references, and indexes for the practicing lawyer. It is not a formal part of any group of divisions.

General

Trade Division

Publishes fiction, humor, biography, art, *belles lettres*, and general nonfiction.

Junior Books Division

Produces children's and young people's books in a wide variety of subjects, as well as educational games and aids.

Encyclopedia and Subscription Books Division

Publishes general and specialized encyclopedias, reference books, and special subscription series.

Educational Technology and Instructional Systems

Text-Film Division

Produces and distributes films, filmstrips, and film loops for the educational and general nonentertainment markets. Both 8 and 16 mm; black and white and color.

Educational Developmental Laboratories, Inc. (a subsidiary)

Designs and produces instructional equipment and associated instructional materials for reading and language arts.

Instructional Systems Division

Designs and publishes integrated multimedia systems of instruction with special emphasis on individualized instruction.

Spitz Laboratories, Inc. (a subsidiary)

Supplies educational institutions and museums in the United States with planetarium classrooms suitable for instruction in environmental, space, earth, and physical sciences.

International Publishing

International Division

Produces English, French, Spanish, and other foreign-language editions of books and materials designed for use in worldwide markets. Publishes in the United States and (in 1968) from six foreign-based subsidiaries with headquarters in the United Kingdom, Canada, Australia, South Africa, Mexico, and Panama.

Foreign Rights Department

The Foreign Rights Department offers McGraw-Hill books to publishers throughout the world for translation into Spanish, Portuguese, Japanese, French, German, Italian, and many other languages. Currently over 3,200 McGraw-Hill titles are in print in over fifty languages. Foreign publishers pay royalties to McGraw-Hill on these translations, and the royalties are shared with the authors.

There are three other major publishing entities in McGraw-Hill, Inc.: McGraw-Hill Publications Division, McGraw-Hill Information Systems Company, and Standard & Poor's. The Publications Division publishes the great majority of McGraw-Hill's magazines and newsletters. F. W. Dodge provides information services and references for the construction industry. Standard & Poor's provides publications and services for the financial and investment community.

INDEX